Addresses on The Temptation

Addresses

on

The Temptation

By
Edward Lee Hicks, M.A.
Canon of Manchester

WIPF & STOCK · Eugene, Oregon

Wipf and Stock Publishers
199 W 8th Ave, Suite 3
Eugene, OR 97401

Addresses on the Temptation
By Hicks, Edward Lee
Softcover ISBN-13: 978-1-7252-9119-5
Hardcover ISBN-13: 978-1-7252-9118-8
eBook ISBN-13: 978-1-7252-9120-1
Publication date 11/2/2020
Previously published by Macmillan and Co., Limited, 1903

This edition is a scanned facsimile of the original edition
published in 1903.

PREFACE.

It is now agreed on all hands, that the secret of Christianity lies in the Personality of Jesus Christ. All else flows therefrom. It is in the hope of discovering this secret, that earnest theologians of every school have begun to focus the lens of criticism upon the Sayings of Christ : these, they assume, must contain the fullest and truest revelation of what He is, for it will be given by Himself.

For many years I have felt that in the story of the Temptation we have a self-revelation of the mind of Christ, embodied in a brief and deeply symbolical narrative, the right interpretation of which—if we could but compass it—would yield invaluable results.

The study of the Temptation involves the question of the supernatural. But again it is obvious, that the miraculous or supernatural in the Gospel centres in the Personality of Christ. When, from a study of the records, we have made up our minds (I speak reverently) who and what He is, we may then enquire whether what is termed the miraculous element in the story befits our conception of Himself.

In my endeavour to interpret one of the most mysterious and significant passages in the Gospel, I have not ventured to ignore two obvious sources of information and suggestion. One of them is the antecedent course of Hebrew religion, and those anticipations of the Messianic Kingdom which certainly coloured the thought and language of Christ. The other is the consentient testimony of the primitive Church, whose earliest writings are admitted to be all but contemporaneous with the events in question. That the constant belief of the Jewish people expected a supernatural Messiah, and that the first generation of Christians regarded Jesus as a supernatural Person, appear to be factors in the problem which it is wise to take into account.

I have, however, honestly endeavoured to lay the chief stress on the ethical and spiritual element, and to deal with the narrative in a spirit of candid enquiry. Some may complain that I dwell unduly upon the Humanity of Christ; others, that I take the supernatural for granted. To the former I reply, that we cannot hope to retain or recover the Catholic faith in Jesus Christ as the central object of the Church's worship, unless we dwell frankly and unreservedly upon His human Epiphany. To the others, I will plead that my view of the essential meaning of the Temptation is independent of any theory of the miraculous, and I have endeavoured to show in what way the supernatural element may be regarded as matter for rational belief.

Neither have I hesitated to speak in the simplest and homeliest terms of the spiritual help afforded us by our Lord's example when under temptation. For, after all, the permanent value of Holy Scripture consists in the comfort and stimulus it supplies to Christian souls in their life-long struggle with evil. What St. Paul said of the Old Testament is far more true of the New, and above all is true of the life and sayings of the Lord: "They were written for our learning, that we through patience and comfort of the Scriptures might have hope" (Rom. xv. 4).

It remains to be said, that these Addresses were preached in Manchester Cathedral on the Fridays in Lent, 1900. Conscious of their imperfections, I have waited in vain amid the distractions of an active life for leisure to revise and re-write them. At last I have had to be content with publishing them almost exactly as they were delivered.

January, 1903.

CONTENTS.

I.
SOME PRELIMINARY THOUGHTS, . . . 1

II.
THE FIRST TEMPTATION, ... 20

III.
THE SECOND TEMPTATION, ... 41

IV.
THE THIRD TEMPTATION, ... 62

V.
THE MYSTERY OF TEMPTATION, . . . 81

VI.
OUR LORD'S USE OF HOLY SCRIPTURE, . 102

THE TEMPTATION OF OUR LORD

I

SOME PRELIMINARY THOUGHTS

"And he was there in the wilderness forty days, tempted of Satan."—St. Mark i. 13.

THE Temptation of our Lord will always remain one of the most interesting and mysterious passages in His wonderful life. It took place in the wilderness of Judaea when He was quite alone. Nobody knew about it but Himself. He was "with the wild beasts," writes St. Mark: alone with nature and with God. It follows that the accounts we have of the Temptation, if authentic, must have come originally from the lips of the Lord Himself. It is a secret experience of Christ, which He thought it best for us to know. May God help us, with due reverence and care, to meditate upon it.

I

The Temptation is recorded in the three Synoptic Gospels, but with characteristic variations. St. Mark, intent upon the outward facts of our Lord's ministry, and following the oral teaching of St. Peter, merely writes: "And immediately the Spirit driveth him into the wilderness. And he was there in the wilderness forty days tempted of Satan; and was with the wild beasts; and the angels ministered unto him." But St. Matthew and St. Luke are concerned to record the discourses as well as the acts of the Lord; they are also deeply interested in the beginnings of His holy life, even before the opening of His ministry; they tell us of His birth, His childhood, of the home at Nazareth. It suits their scheme of narrative to insert a fuller account of the Temptation. Singularly enough, however, the order of the three temptations differs in St. Matthew and St. Luke. In both, indeed, the temptation addressed to His hunger stands first. St. Matthew places next the temptation of the pinnacle, and last the temptation of the mountain. I have little doubt that here the writer follows the original document (on the sayings of Christ) from which the first Gospel is largely derived. St. Luke inverts the order, placing the temptation on the mountain second, and the temptation of the pinnacle third. It was St. Luke's avowed aim to revise the traditional order of the events of the Gospel, reconstructing it on principles of his own.[1] In this particular case his revision has probably corrected an error

[1] See St. Luke's Preface, ch. i. 1 foll., and especially "in order," verse 3.

in the traditional story and has certainly made the mysterious narrative more intelligible. In the fourth Gospel there is no direct mention of the Temptation. This is quite characteristic. The writer studiously omits from his narrative the great events of our Lord's life,—with the marked exception of His Passion and Resurrection, which are the central facts of the Gospel. It is only by way of allusion and reference that he betrays his knowledge of such events as the miraculous Conception, the Birth at Bethlehem, the Transfiguration, the Ascension, or the institution of the two sacraments. Similarly, there is no direct mention of the Temptation in the wilderness. But I think it is alluded to, and (so to say) taken for granted by St. John, when he puts these words into our Lord's mouth in the Garden of Gethsemane (xiv. 30) : " The prince of this world cometh, and hath nothing in me."

A comparison, therefore, of the narratives of the Temptation in the Gospels, leads us to the conviction that in the story of the Temptation we have to do with a primitive document, known perhaps to St. Mark; certainly known to St. Matthew and St. Luke, for the former follows it, and the latter revises it in point of order only. In other words, the narrative of the Temptation is one of the oldest portions of the Gospel story.

But, let us repeat, the ultimate source of the record must of necessity be sought in our Saviour Himself. The Temptation was a secret experience of His spiritual life, which He was pleased to reveal, for our benefit.

The story bears the stamp of truth upon it, in more ways than one. It is authenticated by its simplicity—I had almost said, its crudity of form. It is of a different cast from the narrative in which it is now embedded. It is brief, dramatic, strange. Its compact symbolism does not declare its meaning at once. It may have been but partially understood by the first readers of the Gospel. I have often been inclined to think that the Temptation is one of the least studied and least understood of the events in the Saviour's life. I may be wrong; but that is a chief reason for my choice of it as our subject. I am quite sure that no passage in the Gospel narrative is richer in spiritual teaching.

II

Suggestions of warning and comfort lie indeed on the very surface of the narrative. Let us glance at them as we pass. Thus *Christ was alone* when He was tempted. So we know it is often with ourselves. Satan comes to us with evil thoughts and hideous suggestions, when we are quite alone. He has different modes of attack. Sometimes he finds it easier to prevail, by stirring up other people to tempt us and draw us by bad example, or to frighten us into wrongdoing by ridicule and unkindness. Was it not so with our Lord? "When the temptation"—in the wilderness—"was ended," we read, "Satan departed from him for a season." But Satan was not idle; he did not cease to oppose the mission of the Redeemer. Scribes and Pharisees were incited by him to secret or open antagonism. The weakness of Pilate, the policy of Herod, the passions of the crowd,—nay, the falterings of a Peter or a Thomas, were all employed by the Evil One to baffle and withstand the purpose of Christ. But very often Satan comes upon us suddenly, when we are by ourselves. There is a fallacy in that old hymn,

"And Satan trembles when he sees,
The weakest saint upon his knees."

Solitude, and even prayer, are no safeguard against being tempted. They afford the tempter an opportunity. I have heard of people who think in the same way that their children will be safer from temptation at home than abroad, in the quiet village than in the crowded town. But the truth is, wherever we are, we are liable to temptation. The only safety is in keeping close to the Lord Jesus Christ. Then we shall be able to overcome Satan, whether he attacks us in solitude, or in the company of others.

Note the *time when our Lord was tempted.* He had just been baptized, and the Holy Ghost had come upon Him; He was full of the grace and power of God. No convert of the Baptist had experienced such a crisis before. This flooding of the Saviour's soul by the Spirit was after His baptism, and independent of it. If we seek for analogies to explain it they may be found in the anointing of prophets, priests and kings, or in the ordination service of the Christian Church. Our Lord, at the Jordan, was consecrated by God for His public mission, which began from that hour onward. But if so, then what a strange hour for His temptation! Precisely: that is just how temptation comes to ourselves; just at the hour when we least expect it. Therein lies the craft of the tempter. When you have been at prayer, when you have made new resolves, when you have felt the uplifting of divine grace, when you have taken the Blessed Sacrament,—then beware! For very likely Satan will try to upset you. It will be a grand success for him to take you by surprise and rob you of the good you have got. One has read of the old highway robbers, how they went to work. They always watched for a man who was coming along with plenty of money upon him, a man who had been to market and had been receiving payments. They never cared to stop a poor man. So with the devil, who goes about seeking whom he may devour. It delights him to attack a rich soul, a new convert, a communicant, a Christian worker, a priest of the Church. But, thank God, he need not master us, nor rob us of our blessing: Christ overcame him, and so may we.

III

Why was Christ tempted? There are several answers to this question: let us look at them.

1. He was tempted because He is our brother-man. He came on earth to share our sorrows, and therefore He was "in all things made like unto His brethren" (Heb. ii. 17), and "was in all points tempted like as we are, yet without sin" (Heb. iv. 15). He is our Representative, our Champion. He took upon Himself all the needs, the sorrows, the

responsibilities of humanity. And so, in our name and on our behalf, He had to breast the storm. Here in the wilderness He confronts Satan, our adversary and His.

We know how Milton, when challenged by his quaker-friend Ellwood to treat of Paradise Regained as well as Paradise Lost, found his theme in the Temptation. The evening glories of the poet's genius were devoted to that wonderful story which records how One Man's obedience

"Recovered Paradise to all mankind,
. . . . . .
And Eden raised in the waste wilderness."

Not that Milton conceived of our redemption as achieved in the wilderness rather than on the Cross: nor merely that he saw in the victory of our Lord over the tempter the poetical counterpoise or the logical antithesis to man's primeval surrender; but because in the temptation our Lord stood forth as the personal antagonist of Satan, as the champion of truth against falsehood, of patient goodness against insolent or alluring evil.

There follows from this a most comforting assurance. For it is clear that we may be tempted without sinning; for our Lord Himself had no sin, and yet was tempted. The suggestion to sin came to Him from without, not from within. May it not be so, is it not often so, with ourselves? Sin only begins when we begin to yield to the temptation, and when (even in thought) we wish or feel inclined to do the evil thing which the tempter suggests.

2. He was tempted in order that we might feel assured of His sympathy. The sympathy of some one stronger, wiser, greater than ourselves is always a great help in a difficult struggle.

The raw apprentice, who is trying his best, and finds a great deal in his work that is dull and difficult, is cheered at once if his foreman tells him, " I have gone through it all, my lad, in my time—it's the only way of getting a good training. Go on, and things will be easier soon." The youth in his teens, bewildered and surprised by the new and mysterious impulses that are surging up within him, confusing his conscience, engulfing his will, might be saved from years of sorrow by a word of sympathy from one older than himself. Why do not fathers speak frankly and calmly to their lads at that critical age, and assure them of their knowledge and their perfect sympathy ? What a moral leverage it would confer, what a new power for victory !

Now, in all our troubles and temptations, we have the sympathy of our great Captain and Elder Brother, Jesus Christ. He has overcome the tempter ; and so can we, through Him.

3. We do less than justice to this sacred

experience of Christ, less than justice to His perfect sympathy, if we lay no stress on the reality of His temptation. In a sense, indeed, the conflict was an unequal one, a foregone conclusion. Satan could not really hope to conquer. Mediaeval theology had a curious way of explaining this difficulty. Satan, it suggested, not being omniscient (nor can he be), was unaware of the divinity of Christ; he was deceived and put off his guard by our Lord's humanity. Thus the Redeemer, as the Champion of mankind, challenged the attack of the prince of evil, masking His deity under the human veil. Satan was outwitted: he assailed the Son of man, and was unexpectedly repelled by the Son of God. Thus, said a fanciful interpretation, was answered that mystical question asked of Job (xli. 1, 2): "Canst thou draw out Leviathan with a hook?" What man could not do, Christ did, they said. His humanity was the bait which Leviathan seized, not perceiving the hook for his jaws which lay in our Lord's hidden Godhead.[1] Our enlightened age can endure no such fantastic explanations; we sweep them aside with a smile. But the difficulty remains. We shall perhaps be guided to a right view of our Lord's Temptation (His Temptation not solely in the wilderness, but in the hardships of His troubled life, and finally in Gethsemane and on the Cross) if we fix our thoughts on His sacred humanity. Now the essential characteristic of all that is best in human nature is *growth*. As with the body, so with the mind; the law of life is growth. And not only is this true of the physical and mental faculties; it holds good, even more (if that be possible) of the moral and spiritual powers. They grow by disci-

[1] An interesting account of this idea will be found in Trench's *Sacred Latin Poetry*, p. 167, in the notes on a superb hymn by Adam of St. Victor '*De Resurrectione Domini.*'

pline, by experience, by exercise. It is not merely (even with ourselves) a question of good impulses replacing evil. Our noblest faculties need development and exercise. I know—alas!—that our spiritual growth is far too often a mere matter of repressing sinful passions and crucifying evil habits; through the death of these we make possible the life and growth of Christian virtues. But it is not always so even with us. It was never so with our Redeemer. His pure human soul was as free from sin as a perfect human body would be from the stains of disease.[1] Yet growth and development were the law of His human being. "Jesus grew in wisdom and stature; and in favour with God and

---

[1] It is important to insist on the Christian view, that sin is no essential part of human nature; it is a defect, a corruption. Christ was perfect man, and without sin. The old adage 'humanum est errare' is not wholly true. We realize our true humanity the freer we are made from sin.

SOME PRELIMINARY THOUGHTS

man." His body grew with years, and His strength with regular labour. His mind grew also with teaching and observation. It grew without error, or bias, or prejudice; but it grew, because it was human. He drank in at once and assimilated by unerring intuition all that was true and beautiful in the lessons of nature and of society, in the catechizings of the Rabbis, in the reading of the Law and the Prophets at home and in the synagogue. And so assuredly with His human will and affections. They must needs grow and gather force with exercise. They underwent, indeed, an awful experience. His pure and stainless humanity was to be disciplined by sorrow, matured by conflict, strengthened by endurance, perfected by patience. "Though he were a Son, yet learned he obedience by the things which he suffered" (Heb. v. 8). And therefore He can lend us His perfect sympathy; "For in that he himself hath suffered being tempted, he is able to succour them that are tempted" (Heb. ii. 18). "To him that overcometh will I grant to sit with me in my throne, even as I also overcame, and am set down with my Father in his throne" (Rev. iii. 21).

4. Once again: Christ overcame temptation, to show us the way to overcome. Thrice He defeated the adversary, and how? By a text of Holy Scripture. His whole heart was full of the thought of God, full of the letter and the spirit of the writings that speak of God. And then, when the assault came, it found Him fully armed with the remembrance and love of His Heavenly Father. We must follow that great example. Let us charge our hearts with the love of God and His will, by a habit of prayer and by saturating our minds with Holy Scripture.

The Temptation of our Lord is especially commended by the Church for our meditations in Lent. His fast in the wilderness has determined the duration of this penitential season. The story of the Temptation occupies the Gospel for the First Sunday in Lent, and gives its theme to the Collect.

And therefore I invite you, during the coming weeks, to join me in a frank and devout study of this most profound and yet most profitable passage of the Gospel story.

II

THE FIRST TEMPTATION

"And when the tempter came to him, he said, If thou be the Son of God, command that these stones be made bread. But he answered and said, It is written, Man shall not live by bread alone, but by every word that proceedeth out of the mouth of God."—St. Matt. iv. 3, 4.

We have found the narrative of our Lord's Temptation to have the marks of authentic and primitive tradition. We traced in the very form of the narrative a verification of its truth. It has neither the elaboration nor the obviousness of a later invention. It is the reverse of elaborate; it is crisp, brief, dramatic. It is certainly not

THE FIRST TEMPTATION

obvious; the deep significance of it all is there, when we dive beneath the surface. But the meaning is not obvious, as any one can prove, who tries to teach the Temptation as an intelligible lesson to a class of children. In other words, the narrative comes from an early document, older than the existing gospels, and its ultimate source was the statement of the Saviour Himself.

I do not, however, suppose that the balancing of documentary evidence will have much interest for my present hearers. The literary criticism of the New Testament, and of early Christian writings generally, has indeed great importance and value. It has succeeded in assuring the thinking world that, whatever opinion may be formed of the events narrated in the New Testament, the first Christian documents themselves reach back to a date little if at all later than the events in question.

If any man doubts the Gospel story to-day, it is not for the lack of literary evidence.

I

I imagine that the crux of the problem centres now, as ever, in the question of the supernatural. What evidence is there for the existence of angels, good or evil? What ground have we in reason or nature for accepting the statement of this document (however early), that suggestions of sin were borne in from outside upon a human spirit, and were even pressed upon the consciousness of our sinless Saviour by a spiritual Prince of Evil?

To ask such questions, is to open a large subject, and to go down to the very roots of our Christian faith. I will not say that a man cannot be a good Christian without believing in the devil and his angels. I would welcome as Christ's all who will deny themselves

THE FIRST TEMPTATION

and take up His cross and follow Him. But I cannot conceal from myself, that the Christian tradition from the first accepted the belief of the Jews upon this subject,—purifying that belief indeed and idealizing it perhaps in some particulars, yet accepting it upon the whole as a statement of spiritual fact. To one therefore who doubts the competence of psychology or metaphysics to give an adequate answer to our enquiries respecting moral and spiritual phenomena, and who is ready to accept the guidance of Christ as to the things of God as sufficing at least for present needs, the narrative of the Temptation offers no serious difficulty : and this for three reasons.

1. We must guard ourselves against the delusive antithesis of the terms *natural* and *supernatural*. These adjectives are in fact what a great logician called ' question-begging epithets ' ; they insinuate a fallacy. The spiritual, if it

exists, is as natural as anything else which Divine Wisdom has made and sustains. The true antithesis is between the visible and the invisible, the spiritual and the material. There is absolutely nothing in the facts of nature, as we know them, to forbid our conceiving of spiritual beings, created as we are, yet unlike ourselves in belonging only to a spiritual order of things, and therefore imperceptible by our outward senses. If their existence is affirmed by evidence that claims our respect, there is nothing to hinder our belief. It needs verification, indeed. But it is wholly a question of evidence, and evidence in this kind is confessedly hard to seek. Only we, who are ready to allow the claim of Christ as a Teacher sent from God, —nay, as the Son of God in a supreme and unique sense,—may be willing to accept on His authority the belief in the existence of angelic beings.

2. But our acceptance of our Lord's

authority in this matter does not imply all that it is sometimes thought to imply. Religious humility, as well as intellectual caution, will prevent our deeming the human mind capable of conceiving adequately the conditions of spiritual and suprasensual existence. Not even Christ Himself could have supplied us with adequate ideas on this subject—not because He was unable to impart them, but because we are incapable of receiving them. I assume that the assertions made on the authority of Christ concerning the spiritual world have a real meaning: they represent facts, so far as we are capable of apprehending those facts. But it is possible that when we are translated from this world of sense to the world of spirit, we shall discover that the essential facts themselves are far more wonderful, and far more self-evident, than the faint conceptions we formed of them ever led us to suppose. In other words, the representations of heaven, and judgment, and of angels, from the lips of Christ, are like the descriptions of the great world and its institutions given by a wise and sympathetic adult to a simple, inquisitive child. The representations are true—not absolutely, but relatively; true, not in the literal details of the picture, but in respect of its light and shade and ethical colour. The teaching we have received, I say, is true, and yet may be only the symbol of the spiritual reality. "For now we see by means of a mirror, in a riddle ($\dot{\epsilon}\nu$ $\alpha\dot{\iota}\nu\acute{\iota}\gamma\mu\alpha\tau\iota$): but then face to face."[1]

3. And further, the witness of Scripture to the existence of an external tempter is borne out by our inner experience. Those sudden gusts of passion, those horrible suggestions of evil, those insinuations of doubt, those painful pas-

---

[1] 1 Cor. xiii. 12. Who would now press unduly, as if literal, the dazzling figures of Revelation?

THE FIRST TEMPTATION

sages of our spiritual life in which the whole fabric of our religious belief seems suddenly to totter and fade away, and the very foundations to be cast down—these experiences are painful enough in themselves; but they lose half their horror, and explain themselves in accordance with our inner conviction, if they are really due to the malignity of a tempter, playing upon the weakness and corruption of our hearts. That weakness may be largely due to our own fault, that corruption due to old indulgence in sin, old remissness in duty. Yet we feel that there is a real and actual temptation,—that a spiritual force of evil, not ourselves, is trying to make us its prey.[1]

[1] I am aware that this phenomenon may one day receive some explanation from psychological observation, which already notes the existence of subconscious and semi-conscious conditions in the mind, intruding upon the consciousness.

II

There is another question which a thoughtful reader of the narrative is always inclined to ask, and which demands some kind of answer—I mean the question, How could the sinless Christ be, in any real sense, capable of temptation? To this enquiry some reply was attempted in my first Address. But the difficulty is so commonly felt, and involves so much within it, that I feel bound to offer one or two further suggestions.

1. The attack of Satan was made not along the avenues of any gross or sinful desires, nor in the direction of any manifest evil. We shall perceive, as we study the several temptations, that the assault is directed upon certain elementary needs or impulses of our nature, which were essential factors of our Lord's humanity. These needs and impulses are in themselves abso-

lutely innocent, they are simply human. Certainly they can easily be made the opportunity or instrument of sin, and in a sinful nature they are frequently turned to the service of evil. But of themselves they are not sinful; they are, at the worst, neutral or indifferent. The whole question of right or wrong depends on the direction our character gives them, the use we make them to serve.

2. Again, the attack of Satan is veiled under the guise of religion and of principle; "If thou be the Son of God." He calls evil good, and good evil, and so subtly that it almost appears to be so. He lies, as ever, but so dexterously that there is half a truth mingled with the falsehood:

"Some truth there was, but mashed and brewed
    with lies,
To tickle fools and puzzle half the wise."

So perplexed, so interwoven in the

Temptation of our Lord is the problem of right and wrong, that the disentanglement of truth and error demanded no less penetration of judgment than delicacy of conscience. We know not (I speak with all reverence) whether more to admire the keen intellectual insight or the simple filial submission of our Redeemer in His replies to the Tempter.

3. But further, it is clear that our Lord's sojourn in the wilderness was for the purpose of prayer and meditation, for self-recollection. This is not stated in so many words by the evangelists. They simply insert, without explanation or paraphrase, the primitive record, that He "went into the wilderness to be tempted." But the truth is, our Lord's temptation occurred in the very process and current of His meditation. His prayer and His meditation had for their object the duties and difficulties of His impending mis-

sion. These duties and difficulties He will deliberately look at all round, and examine in all their bearings. He will measure His task, and take stock of His powers, and forecast His methods and principles of action. It is in the very course of this meditation that the Temptation occurred. The Temptation could not (it seems to us) have come at all, but that our Lord's thoughts were already bent in this direction. His close examination of His approaching task gave opportunity to the Tempter to suggest a wrong method of attempting it. His suggestion formed one of several alternatives, that had to be canvassed and rejected in favour of that course which represented the will of the Father. '

III

Let us look a little closer at our great theme. We read that as soon as our

Lord was baptized, and was filled with the Holy Spirit, "Then the Spirit driveth him into the wilderness." He went, therefore, in obedience to a divine call, a spiritual impulse. If we enquire closely into this call, we shall be able to understand in some measure the reason of it. We might, perhaps, have expected our Lord, as soon as He was filled with the Spirit, to begin preaching and teaching, and doing wonderful works. But we find him doing nothing of the kind. His first step is into the wilderness. Instead of seeking company, He seeks solitude; instead of beginning work, He fasts and prays.

We hardly need pause to observe that this is the right way of beginning any great work of God. Let us be in no hurry. Let us prepare ourselves by prayer and meditation beforehand. Thus did Christ, spending forty days of fasting and prayer in the wilderness,

THE FIRST TEMPTATION

before He opened His public mission amongst men. And this is the way of His great saints also. Moses, by God's providence, spent one third of a lifetime in the desert of Midian, to prepare him for the work of delivering Israel. He spent forty days and nights on Sinai, alone with God, before receiving the Law to give to God's people. St. Paul after his conversion, and before he began his missionary travels, "went into Arabia" (Gal. i. 17), and spent there the best part of three years in solitude, working out prayerfully and logically the great problem of the status of the Gentiles in the Christian Church, and measuring the difficulty and danger of asserting such a doctrine. And so with ourselves. We must find time for prayer. A quiet time spent alone with God is the best preparation for every work we have to do for Him. Thus let every day begin with prayer, with really heartfelt converse with God.

As good George Herbert so quaintly sings:

> "Sum up at night, what thou hast done by day;
> And in the morning, what thou hast to do.
> Dress and undress thy soul: mark the decay
> And growth of it: if, with thy watch, that too
> Be down, then wind up both: since we shall be
> Most surely judged, make thy accounts agree."

We may truly say that our Lord withdrew into solitude to think out His work beforehand, to settle its principles, to determine its methods. In the course of His public ministry, which was now to begin, all sorts of problems and perplexities would confront Him. His life henceforward would be full of conflicts and temptations. Was it not wiser for Him (we may reverently say), and was it not better, to meet these questions and conflicts beforehand, and so settle His course once for all? It we look attentively at the temptations of Christ, we shall discover that they were the very temptations which He

THE FIRST TEMPTATION

met with all along the course of His ministry. Let us see how this appears.

The first temptation was the temptation of hunger. "And when he had fasted . . . he was afterward an hungered" (St. Matt. iv. 2). Our Lord would often have to be hungry. He was going to lead a life of absolute poverty. We reflect that until now He had a house of His own at Nazareth, and a carpenter's shop, and a regular trade; so that, though He was only a working man without any prominence in the world, yet He was able to maintain Himself and a widowed mother in the refined simplicity and tender peace of the Nazareth home. But all this was now to cease,—He was to have no more a regular home, no more a fixed employment. He would truly not have where to lay His head, and He would have to depend for daily bread upon the kindness of friends like Lazarus, and on the offerings of holy women like Mary

Magdalene, and Joanna, and Susanna, wife of Chuza, Herod's steward, and others who believed in His claims. In plain words, He was to be homeless and penniless. He was about to forego deliberately the happiness of home, the comfort of regular earnings. For reasons I will not here dwell upon, but chiefly because the pride of wealth was a crying sin of His country and His time, and because the gulf between rich and poor is the social chasm which in all ages Christian charity would have to endeavour to span, and could only span by love of others and sacrifice of self,—therefore would Christ Himself abstain wholly from all property, and impose the same rule of abstinence upon His twelve disciples. No wonder that we read of His being weary with His journey, and sitting hungry and thirsty at the well. No wonder that one day His disciples were glad to pluck the ears of the corn they

THE FIRST TEMPTATION 37

passed through, and to eat them, rubbing them in their hands. No wonder that, when He fed the thousands in the wilderness, He bade the disciples "gather up the fragments that remain, that nothing be lost"; for He and the twelve were thankful to have the broken food, the leavings of the multitude, to supply their own worse needs.

Now because our Lord would have to bear this burden of poverty all through His ministry, therefore He chose to experience the full weight of it at the first. He retires, like His Forerunner and many an earlier saint, into the Judaean wilderness, to forego the comforts of life, to endure hardness, to be alone with God and nature, and to live for a while on the scanty provision of the desert, locusts and wild honey perhaps, and water from the spring, and berries from the bush. In this temptation He is fighting His battle beforehand. But Satan, amid His hunger, suggests a thought of misgiving, a doubt of discontent. 'Was it right and reasonable for the Son of God, One whom God so loved, One who had such an august commission, to be in want of bread? What good could it do to any one? What good could it do to Himself?' . . . "If thou be the Son of God, command that these stones be made bread."

It sounded very plausible,—Satan's suggestions always do. It sounded both reasonable and kindly. Yet it struck at the roots of that holy life.

For, remember, our Lord was hungering by the will of God. His Father's guidance had brought Him thither. He was preparing Himself by the voluntary privations of the wilderness for the inevitable privation that was to follow. He is quite content with privation and hunger, either now or then, if that be His Father's will, and He is persuaded that so it is. To be hungry was no proof that the Father did not love His

THE FIRST TEMPTATION 39

Son. He was not the only child of God who had been in need, and had to depend, even for daily bread, upon the love and providence of God. God had once led His son Israel (Ex. iv. 22) into the wilderness, "a land that was not sown," and when that son was hungry and thirsty God had provided bread and water in abundance in answer to his prayer, with rebuke also for his lack of faith. And so our Lord replies, in words (Deut. viii. 3) spoken first concerning Israel in the wilderness : " It is written, Man shall not live by bread alone, but by every word that proceedeth out of the mouth of God." That is, no matter what hunger, and want, and poverty befal us, if only we trust ourselves in the hands of our Father like true children, and regard His Word of command as a promise, as our comfort and stay. For here, as elsewhere, hunger is typical of all the elementary needs of life. Just as when our Lord taught us to pray to our Father in heaven, "Give us this day our daily bread," that one temporal petition sums up in itself all our bodily needs,—so here in our Lord's Temptation this pang of His hunger assures of His complete sympathy with us, His fellow-sufferers, in every privation and necessity, and disappointed desire. And He tells us, by His own example, how to meet the trial : " It is written, Man shall not live by bread alone." Enough, if God's will be the centre of our life and being. This was the temper of our Saviour's spirit always : " My meat is to do the will of him that sent me, and to finish his work" (St. John iv. 34).

III

THE SECOND TEMPTATION

"Again, the devil taketh him up into an exceeding high mountain, and sheweth him all the kingdoms of the world, and the glory of them; and saith unto him, All these things will I give thee, if thou wilt fall down and worship me. Then saith Jesus unto him, Get thee hence, Satan: for it is written, Thou shalt worship the Lord thy God, and him only shalt thou serve."—ST. MATT. iv. 8-10.

THE second temptation, according to St. Matthew, was the temptation on the pinnacle. But the order given by St. Luke seems most in accord with the spiritual significance of the awful transaction. We therefore follow St.

Luke's order and deal next with the temptation on the mountain.

I

Observe that, whereas the first temptation came through the body and its needs, the second temptation has to do with the soul's desire. It bears on the work of Christ in relation to others. It is not necessary to believe that our Lord was bodily removed from the wilderness and placed upon a mountain summit. Indeed, it is obvious that there is no mountain-height in the world, Alpine or Himalayan, that would afford a view of "all the kingdoms of the world, and the glory of them." We may rest assured that what is here described is a vision. It was in thought that our Lord was transported to a mountain-top, and surveyed the glories of the world; for 'thought is quick.'

No words of mine are needed to help our imagination to conceive what that vision was, and all it may have involved. Enough, and perhaps more than enough, has been done for us in this regard by the magnificent descriptions of Milton. For the child Jesus had seen little of the world's splendour; He had been reared in the seclusion of Nazareth. The beauty and change of field and sky, the song of birds, the play of human character and motive, the vicissitudes of life, all these He knew by long and sympathetic experience. But His only knowledge of a great city came through the pilgrim-visits to Jerusalem, and joining in the national festivals. Yet almost under the walls of Nazareth the caravans of merchants and travellers passed daily on their way from Arabia and the far East, bound for Judaea and Egypt, and the fairs of the south and west. The murmurs of the movements of the great world reached even the peasants of the Galilean hill-sides. They could measure the greatness of the great world-powers when they reflected that the Herods, whose rule they found so severe, and even Herod the Great who had rebuilt Jerusalem and its temple, had all of them been no more than the servants, and even the puppets of that awful Cæsar, who sat in solemn majesty in the palace of far-off Rome, controlling at his will the government of the world. And the Galilean peasants—and not the least our Divine Lord among them—as they mused upon the movements of the world, and the coming and going of kings and legates, brought to their meditation hearts full of the words and thoughts of the great prophets and psalmists of their race. "The Lord is King, be the people never so impatient." "The meek-spirited shall possess the earth: and shall be refreshed in the multitude of peace" (Ps. xcix. 1; xxxvii. 11).[1]

[1] The *Magnificat* seems to give utterance to some such thoughts: "He hath showed strength

II

The second temptation of our Lord is one that could only come to a strong, gifted and aspiring nature. It is the temptation of ambition, of genius that is becoming conscious of its powers. For our Lord had been born into the world as man, that He might be a king and leader of men. He was to bring about a moral revolution, to establish a spiritual kingdom. "Art thou a king, then?" said Pilate; and our Lord replied frankly, "Thou sayest that I am a king." But He adds, "My kingdom is not of this world; else would my servants fight." Now there are only two ways of obtaining ascendancy and leadership

with his arm: he hath scattered the proud in the imagination of their hearts. He hath put down the mighty from their seat": *i.e.* the greatest powers of the world, even that of Rome, shall be humbled before Israel's God and His Messiah, who now is coming.

among men; it must either be by force or by persuasion,—by the sword, or by moral and intellectual influence. We know which method appealed to the imagination of the ordinary Jew. He hoped for a repetition of the glorious struggle of the Maccabees, in which the Roman army should be destroyed, and the Messianic Kingdom at last established on Mount Zion. But Christ from the first deliberately set this dream aside. His was to be a spiritual kingdom.

This then was the task that lay before our Lord: to win the moral homage of the world; to bring mankind to follow His leadership, to rely on His love and promise, to own His sovereign claims. And here in the wilderness He measures the vastness of the task. He, the peasant-prophet of Nazareth,—homeless, unsupported, without followers, without resources, nay, without so much as human learn-

THE SECOND TEMPTATION 47

ing, as men count learning,—how is He to win the attention of mankind, and to secure and retain their obedience?

There are some natures gifted with a magnetic power of attraction for other men. They are so simple, so unselfish, so frank, and withal so strong, that we trust them at once; and their ideas are so fresh, their convictions so clear, and their mode of expression so vivid and surprising, that it is a happiness to be in their company. All this, and very much more, was true of our blessed Lord. He was, and is, the Teacher of men. There is no love like His love, no thoughts so original, no speech so illuminating, so compelling, as His. "The common people heard him gladly," we read (St. Mark xii. 37). "Never man spake like this man," said the untutored officers (St. John vii. 46). "Lord, to whom shall we go? thou hast the words of eternal life, and we believe and are sure that thou art that Christ, the son of the living God," was the avowal of St. Peter (St. John vi. 68-69). Every supreme genius is conscious of its powers. Our Saviour was no exception. Perhaps He scarcely realized as yet what form those powers would take, what extent they would have, what place they would occupy in His public ministry. But whatever powers and gifts were His by the endowment of the Holy Spirit who was outpoured on Him without measure, these He was eager to employ, for the glory of God and the benefit of men.

But whoever be the teacher and leader, and however great his powers, there lies before him the dread certainty that human prejudice and blindness and folly can defeat the best endeavours. No man can be convinced of error, or reclaimed from sin against his will.

THE SECOND TEMPTATION

Our Lord "knew what was in man." He could foresee, before He came to actual experience, how strong is prejudice, how hard is pride, how cruel is religious hate. Any great and original teacher, conscious of his powers, can easily perceive that his success will depend not so much upon the willing converts he may make among those who are ready for his coming, as on the skill and address with which he can beguile the unwilling hearer, and melt the ice of prejudice. Here is the real difficulty of every reformer and prophet. A large part of the world is never ready to hear the teachings of purity, mercy and truth. "The whole world lieth in the wicked one," wrote St. John, sadly.[1] Satan has obtained a vast influence over human nature. Men's souls are far too much under

[1] Ἐν τῷ πονηρῷ. The phrase is a remarkable one, and should be compared with the close of the Lord's Prayer; see p. 98.

the influence of the world, the flesh and the devil; and where these are dominant the voice of Christ cannot be heard. It is at this point that the second temptation of our Lord becomes so simple, so terrible a fact. If Satan has obtained so large an influence over human nature, if human minds are so perverted by passion and prejudice, by interest or by ignorance, it may be necessary for the teacher of truth to make allowance for man's obliquity, and "to catch them with guile." This phrase was invented by St. Paul, a very prince of teachers.[1] And certainly all wise and sympathetic educators will proceed on this plan. It was Christ's way. He taught His disciples the truth by degrees "as they were able to hear it" (St. Mark iv. 33). By degrees He broke to them the terrible secret that He would have

[1] 2 Cor. xii. 16: the language is playful, of course.

THE SECOND TEMPTATION

to be rejected, and suffer, and die. Few things indeed in the Gospel story are more pathetic than the patience of our Lord with the blindness, the dulness, the perverse misapprehension of the twelve. So far, however, all is wise and right. This method of patience, and of the gradual imparting of knowledge, every good and loving teacher will adopt. But then rushes in the hideous temptation for the teacher: "Shall I wrap up my lesson and hide away some part of the truth for fear of my scholars being frightened away?" If so, how far may the teacher go in leaving things unsaid that might be taken amiss? How far may he go in humouring the prejudices of the hearers? May he not win them with guile first, and then hope presently to teach them more fully the truth? "Certainly," strikes in Satan at this point. "Acknowledge my power over human souls. Realize that you cannot teach perfect or absolute truth, for most men will never believe it. Teach half the truth, and be happy to have done so much. You cannot teach perfect morality, or perfect purity, or perfect justice, for men will never practise it. Don't pitch your standard too high for human nature, or else human nature will rebel. Remember that I, Satan, have such wide influence, such deep-seated power over human nature, that you will never make it really good. Compromise with evil. Accommodate yourself to human sin. Recognize my power ; do not exclude my influence from human nature, and then your task will be simple. Disciples will be many ; the world will applaud. It will see that it has not to deal with a mere fanatic, a dreamer, but with a wise and practical man, who understands human nature, and is willing to compromise with forces of evil which are manifestly invincible. 'If thou wilt fall down and worship me, all will be thine.'"

III

To the ordinary reader, the third temptation appears the strangest of all. How could Satan for an instant suppose that the Lord would bow down and worship him? In other words, how could it be a real temptation to our Redeemer to recognize the authority of the devil? How can such a thing be conceivable?

The explanation of the third temptation that has been here suggested, will show it to be real and natural enough. The spirit of compromise is everywhere in the world. It prompts us to be silent when we ought to speak, for fear of offending; to praise, when it is not deserved, to keep people our friends; to tolerate sin, and not to remonstrate, because it might make us enemies. It is in this spirit that churches have condoned wickedness in high places, for fear of man. The minister accepts the money of the brewer, and then is lukewarm about temperance reform. The owner of slum property is tolerated as a church-officer, and the whole church becomes guilty of conniving at his selfishness. It was thus with the question of slavery in the United States before the war of secession. Whole churches tolerated slavery, against their better conscience, because it seemed impossible to break with the slave-holders. Similar problems harass us to-day. How far ought a parish priest to go in enlightening his people as to the admitted results of Old Testament criticism? If he speaks, he may terribly offend weaker brethren; if he is silent, he is untrue to his conscience, and exposes his younger people to the danger of intellectual revolt against religion when they arrive at the age and opportunity of reflection and enquiry. How far, again, is a man, and especially a preacher, to be silent if he differs from his fellows on the present war policy?[1] Ought he to be silent and cloak his conviction, or speak and expose himself to insult or peril? Or the young man of business who finds customs in his trade that revolt his sense of truth—what is he to do? to acquiesce, for the sake of a living, or to forsake all and follow Christ?

There is no end of examples; they abound throughout our daily experience. The spirit of immoral compromise can always be detected by the cant phrases it affects; such as "It's of no use trying to alter it"; "They all do it"; "It is the custom of the trade"; "One must live"; "Don't be a faddist"; "The idea is Utopian." These, and others like them, are the stock phrases of the baser sort

[1] This was written in the spring of 1900.

of the worldly-wise. They all amount to this confession, that evil is too strongly entrenched to be uprooted; it must be tolerated. And, further, that if you want to get on in the world you must not be over-precise, or you will lose your influence, and then you will do no good at all. What is this but the very suggestion of Satan: "All this power will I give thee; . . . for that is delivered unto me; and to whomsoever I will I give it. If thou therefore wilt worship me, all shall be thine" (St. Luke iv. 6-7).

Our Lord flings back the suggestion with horror: "Get thee hence, Satan!" and He adds: "It is written, Thou shalt worship the Lord thy God, and him only shalt thou serve." On that principle our Saviour went to work always as the Teacher and Redeemer of men. He was intolerant of evil, wherever He found it. All-merciful to the sinner, He was unsparing of the

THE SECOND TEMPTATION

sin. He never feared to give offence. He scandalized and outraged the respectable and religious classes by His words and deeds. He ate with publicans, He was familiar with outcasts, He spoke kindly to and of Samaritans; He denounced the Pharisees as hypocrites, and the Scribes as formalists. To His believing followers He spoke so strongly and strangely of the eating of His body and His blood, that many said, "That is a hard saying," and left Him for ever; so that He appealed to His twelve with the question, "Will ye also go away?" He told the rich young ruler "to sell all that he had and give to the poor," so that he went away sorrowing, "for he had great possessions." He insisted on the necessity of cross-bearing, and told His friends and followers not to dream of a literal and temporal kingdom. He braved misconception and calumny, He dared opposition and hate, and He crowned His mission with the cross. He had treated Satan all along as an enemy, spurning all compromise; He had never yielded an inch to him. And so the world seemed lost, and not won; Jesus was crucified, and Satan triumphed. Was it really so? We know far otherwise.

The willing and adoring homage of the noblest and best of men, the worship of the most cultured and progressive nations of mankind are offered at this moment to our Lord in ever-widening numbers, just because He was true to the Father that sent Him, true to the Truth, true to Himself. And because He died for the truth, therefore He rose again, and ascended into heaven, and reigns for ever as the Saviour and Lord of all that are loyal and true to Him and to His righteousness.

IV

My friends, the progress of mankind and the real bettering of the world depend wholly upon our individual loyalty to truth. The spirit of compromise is the handmaid of reaction, and herald of decline. In the words of our most thoughtful statesman : " Progress depends upon tendencies and forces in a community. But of these tendencies and forces the organs and representatives must plainly be found among the men and women of the community, and cannot be found anywhere else. Progress is not automatic, in the sense that if we were all to be cast into a deep slumber for the space of a generation, we should awake to find ourselves in a greatly improved social state. The world only grows better even in the moderate degree in which it grows better, because people wish that it should, and take the right and proper steps to make it better. Evolution is not a force, but a process; not a cause, but a law. It explains the source, and marks the immovable limitations of social energy. But social energy itself can never be superseded by evolution or by anything else. The reproach of being impracticable and artificial attaches by right not to those who insist on resolute, persistent, and uncompromising efforts to remove abuses, but to a very different class—to those, namely, who are credulous enough to suppose that abuses and bad customs and wasteful ways of doing things will remove themselves. This credulity, which is a cloak for indolence or ignorance or stupidity, overlooks the fact that there are bodies of men, more or less numerous, attached by every selfish interest they have to the maintenance of these abusive customs."[1]

And therefore we conclude that the

[1] Mr. John Morley, *On Compromise*, p. 161.

THE SECOND TEMPTATION

second temptation is a very practical matter for us. Every one of us is in danger of giving up the struggle with evil. We are tempted to let things be; to give up trying to alter them. We drift into easy-going ways. We wink at sin, and make a compromise with evil, at times because we are afraid of man, at times because we are thinking of our pockets. But whatever the motive, it means this,—we allow that Satan is too strong to be interfered with; that the world in part belongs to him, and he cannot be dispossessed; that life cannot be lived with comfort or advantage unless we make terms with him. And this is precisely what he asked our Lord to do. "Bow down . . . and all shall be thine." But this is precisely what we do not mean to do, for our Lord did not. We will take His cross as our standard; in this sign we shall conquer. "He shall bruise Satan under your feet shortly."

IV

THE THIRD TEMPTATION

"And he brought him to Jerusalem, and set him on a pinnacle of the temple, and said unto him, If thou be the Son of God, cast thyself down from hence: for it is written, He shall give his angels charge over thee, to keep thee: and in their hands they shall bear thee up, lest at any time thou dash thy foot against a stone."—
St. Luke iv. 9-11.

WE come now to the third temptation. As was remarked of the second temptation, so we may say here, that it is wholly unnecessary to suppose that our Lord was bodily removed from the wilderness and literally placed upon the summit of the temple. The transaction

THE THIRD TEMPTATION

took place in the spiritual sphere. It was terribly real as a temptation, yet the circumstances and surroundings existed only as a matter of inner and spiritual vision. But, indeed, we mistake the meaning of the word 'real' when we suppose it to signify the material and the sensible. The spiritual is the real.

The third temptation, then, was a purely spiritual temptation. It was more completely so, if that were possible, than the other two.

I

For the first temptation sprang out of the sufferings of the body: it was a temptation of the flesh. It was an acute form of that external poverty which our Lord would have to endure all through His suffering life.

And the second temptation was a temptation of the world. It found its occasion, that is, in our Lord's relations with humanity at large; it arose out of His claims upon their regard; out of His desire for their salvation; out of His hopes and plans of winning their love and obedience. The tempter would play upon Christ's love of mankind, and entice Him to vary His standard of inflexible truth and goodness, in order to conciliate the weakness of men. Our Saviour resisted: it was a temptation of the world.

But the third and last temptation had no reference to the sufferings of the bodily frame, nor to the feelings and opinions of the rest of mankind. It was neither a temptation of the flesh nor of the world: it was a temptation of the spirit. It had to do simply with the inner consciousness of Christ Himself, in relation only to the Father. It was a temptation which derived its force from the high and glorious powers possessed by the Saviour as the Anointed Son of Man. He had become man for our sakes; He had humbled Himself to the lowest station, and to uttermost poverty. He had sacrificed all for man. But He is still very God of very God, begotten of the Father before all worlds; by whom all things were made. And, further, in His human nature, He has just been filled with the Holy Ghost at Jordan, and assured of the presence and power of the Father to accomplish the work of redemption. That work He was now openly to begin by a public ministry. He is conscious at once of weakness and of power; of utter weakness and of almighty power. He is indeed utterly weak; none can be poorer, weaker, lonelier. But He is strong also; strong not only in the almighty power of His deity, which He has veiled in the flesh; but strong also in the strength of the Father's unspeakable love for men whom He is to redeem; strong with the strength of the Holy Spirit, who dwells in Him "without measure." Nothing can be impossible to Him. All power to bless, to soothe, to save, is assured to Him. No human suffering, no human grief, can be beyond His power to comfort or remove. Whatever power of doing wonderful works had been permitted in olden days to a Moses, a Samuel, an Elijah or Elisha, would surely be His. Nothing could be too hard for Him if it were necessary for the salvation of man, for the working out of God's purpose of the world's redemption.

As yet, we remember, our Blessed Lord had not done any wonderful work; His life had been one of the quietest and humblest in the world. Self-repression, self-humiliation, had been its keynote; He had emptied Himself of His glory. But henceforward all the latent forces of spiritual dominion were to be called into action;

no power, no faculty that He could employ for the bettering of mankind and the glorifying of God was to lie unused. What He could do He was now to do for the overcoming of evil.

Yes,—for the overcoming of evil. That was the one sole purpose for which He had come into the world. For this sole object He possessed, and should employ, mysterious and superhuman powers.

II

And now, in the light of this thought, look again at this third temptation of Satan. He reminds the Saviour of the promises of God. In the merciful task which he had undertaken, was He not sure of the Father's blessing? Certainly He might appropriate the beautiful assurances of Psalm xci. : " Whoso dwelleth under the defence of the Most High, shall abide under the shadow of the Almighty."

He was encompassed by divine love, upborne by divine power, led by divine guidance, indwelt and animated by the divine Spirit. He might well yield Himself to the delightful consciousness of power, and taste the rapture of His glorious privilege. Danger itself might well be courted, for the very delight of proving His mysterious powers, and risks might be joyfully run for the sheer pleasure of feeling the comfort and glory of divine support. Nay, would it not be doing honour to the Father that sent Him, thus to cast Himself upon the divine protection? "Cast thyself down. . . . He shall give his angels charge concerning thee, and in their hands they shall hold thee up, lest thou dash thy foot against a stone."

Pride is the devil's own sin. It is said to have caused his expulsion from heaven. But pride, spiritual pride, is also the sin of the saint. To be lifted up with the sense of God's love, and to glory in it as if God could not do without us, and as if we were the favourite children of God's great family —that is spiritual pride. It is the temptation not of the sinner, but of the saint. "I am saved; God loves me; God's grace upholds me; I am so happy! God be praised for His goodness;"—such feelings and expressions as these are good and right. But all depends on what they lead up to. What is the next thing for us to say and do? Is it: "Lord, help me therefore to watch and pray, lest I abuse my blessing, lest I forfeit Thy love, lest I grow slack in my duties." If that be our attitude, all is well. But if there steals into our souls the feeling that somehow God will take care of us, and that His love is such that He will let no harm befal us, so that we watch the less, because God will watch the more; and do less, because God will do all; and indulge our inclinations a little, for God will shield us from ill; and risk danger, since God takes such loving care;—if this be the secret and half-unconscious trend of our thoughts, then great is our peril. For this is Satan coming to us, as he came to the Saviour, to tell us that God loves us so much, that we may cast ourselves down, for all will be well. Very sternly our Saviour flung back the suggestion of the Evil One. "It is written: Thou shalt not tempt the Lord thy God."

What does this answer mean? It means simply this: that God's love and favour are indeed ours, and we may well be happy to possess them. But we possess them only so long as we remain humble, obedient, and submissive children of God. So soon as we are proud of God's love, His smile becomes a frown. To be proud of God's favour is to lose it. Humbly to rejoice in God's love, that is the best way of retaining it. Very quietly to do God's will, is the way to make sure of His grace. We may not tempt the Lord our God.

When Israel, God's son of old, came out of Egypt, it was wholly through God's love and favour. In the wilderness Israel could find no water to drink, and behaved like a spoilt child, complaining that God should have allowed them to come into such a difficulty. God gave them water out of the rock—the best water, and in plenty.

But with the water came also the rebuke. "Ye shall not tempt the Lord your God" (Deut. vi. 16). That is, they were like spoilt children; they had been so lovingly treated, that they thought God was bound to give them everything they wanted, and oblige their every whim. They were puffed up with their privileges; they had grown proud of their mercies. Thereby they tempted God to withdraw His favours from them.

III

If any being in the universe had a right to rejoice in the possession of God's love and favour, and repose calmly in the sense of that possession, that Being was the Saviour. Yet what do we find? Instead of rejoicing and triumphing in the possession of unique privileges, we find Him constant in prayer, exhibiting always the greatest humility and submission, and seldom making use of His supernatural powers. One of the most wonderful facts of our Lord's wonderful life is this—His strict economy of power, His frugality in the employment of miraculous force.

He never works a miracle to comfort Himself. For others He will make water into wine to prevent embarrassment at a village wedding, and will multiply bread in the wilderness rather than let a crowd risk the pangs of hunger. But for Himself it is enough to gather up the leavings of the food— "the fragments that are left"; just as, at Jacob's Well, He is content to beg a woman to give Him a draught of water, and will wait till His disciples return from buying some bread. His miracles are for others' comfort, not His own. "He saved others; Himself He cannot save."

But further, what an absence of show and of pomp there is in His wonderful works! They are done so quietly, so gently. He Himself commonly begs the recipient of the benefit not to speak of it, not to make it known. It is true that it cannot be hid. The news leaks out, and causes wide excitement. Yet nearly every miracle seems to appeal rather to our sympathy than to our wonder; it speaks to us more of the Lord's compassion than of His power. He appears to have been pained when His disciples allowed themselves merely to wonder at His miracles; they ought, He implies, to have seen in them something deeper, more spiritual than this. "When the disciples saw it they marvelled, saying, 'How soon is the fig-tree withered away!' Jesus answered and said unto them, 'Verily I say unto you, If ye have faith, and doubt not, ye shall not only do this which is done to this fig-tree, but also if ye shall say unto this mountain, Be thou removed, and be thou cast into the sea; it shall be done'" (Matt. xxi. 20-21). It is simply extraordinary to reflect how little our Lord rested His claims on mere wonder-working. His miracles were indications of His nature, signs of His love as well as of His power, proofs that God's great mercy was really active in the world—healing its sores, relieving its sorrows, lightening the burdens of weary humanity. That surely is the impression conveyed by the Gospel story. Indeed, nothing so staggers us in the whole course of our Saviour's career as the contrast between His majestic authority and His meek bearing, between His glorious power and His humble ways. Never were such mighty forces so gently used, and the inexhaustible resources of omnipotence so sparingly employed.

IV

Here then is a plain and impressive lesson for every Christian soul. We are so easily inclined to be gratified by God's love for us instead of being simply thankful. We are so liable to be lifted up when we find ourselves succeeding by the power of God,—like the seventy when they came back to Christ and exclaimed with childlike glee, "Lord, even the devils are subject unto us through Thy name!" And our Lord replied: "In this rejoice not that the spirits are subject unto you; but rather rejoice, because your names are written in heaven." That is, let them rejoice without pride; let them avoid raptures, if raptures tend to put them off their spiritual balance. Dutiful obedience is better than rapturous joy. The best attitude of the Christian is a quiet waiting upon God.

Nothing is more extraordinary and insidious than the temptation of spiritual pride. It is like a blight that attacks our best efforts in the bloom. It is a sort of parasite that fastens on our virtues as they ripen. How hard it is to be really humble, and how easy it is to be proud of our humility! Nothing can be more widely contrasted than the Pharisee and the Publican in our Lord's parable. And yet how fatally easy is it for the prayer of the penitent—"God be merciful to me a sinner"—to lose itself insensibly in the

THE THIRD TEMPTATION 77

Pharisee's rapture, " Lord, I thank thee that I am not as other men are!"

The other day I had a letter from a young man who once was on the brink of a terrible sin, but was mercifully recovered just in time, and who has won so far a noble victory by watching and praying. He asked me for advice about Confession, for he had felt an inclination to make confession to a priest before Easter;—" did I advise him to do so, or not?" I replied by telling him that if he had any spiritual difficulty, or if he could not obtain a clear conscience and rid himself of the sense of guilt, then it was his plain duty to avail himself of that wholesome medicine for sick souls which the Church so frankly and lovingly offered. But I begged him to observe, that the benefit of Absolution upon private Confession was not to be sought because of its joy or comfort, but rather in order to brace the soul for more effective service of God. In other words Confession is not a cordial, but a tonic.

Religion, it is certain, affords many exquisite pleasures,—some of them, I imagine, among the keenest delights that human nature can experience. But I think our Lord's behaviour under this Third Temptation may help us better to measure the value of religious comforts, and more wisely to use them. Sometimes we are transported with the sense of the corporate life of the Church, when our voices join in glorious psalm or hymn, and music dissolves our heart in ecstasies. Sometimes it is the delicate grace of historic ritual with its association with the saintliness of older days, that kindles the religious emotion. Sometimes, again, it is the passionate or convincing voice of the preacher. Yet let us bear in mind, always and everywhere, that the delights of religion are not its vital part. Emotion may come and go, and the sensible comforts of religion may be denied us. But what is essential is the life, the character, the conduct: what we are, not what we feel. For the offering of worship to God is a sacrifice, if it is to be anything at all; and every sacrifice must be salted with the salt of self-denial. And the pulpit exists for the guidance of conscience, for the strengthening of purpose; and the Sacraments are given for the conferring of grace; and grace and guidance are ours, not for the joy of knowing the right nor for the blissful consciousness of power to do it, but that we may better serve God and our neighbour, and do the Lord's will.

Not without reason did our Lord (following the suggestion of the prophet Ezekiel [1]) choose the Vine as the type of the Church in respect of her spiritual life. For in the vine there is little of form to delight us, and still less of colour, and the flower of the vine almost eludes the eye though we may

[1] Ezekiel xv.

perceive its fragrance ; for all the glories of form and of colour, of fragrance and beauty, are reserved for the fruit alone ; in that the vine reigns pre-eminent : " Herein is my Father glorified, that ye bear much fruit : so shall ye be my disciples." Not raptures, nor upliftings of the soul, not feelings, but conduct and action,—these are what God demands.

Even when we pass to the innermost experiences of the spiritual life, there is room for self-denial; even there the Cross must be borne. " A true lover of Christ " (says the author of the *Imitatio*), " and a diligent follower of virtue, does not fall back on comforts, nor seek such sensible sweetnesses ; but rather prefers hard exercises, and to sustain severe labours for Christ. . . . When consolation is taken from thee, do not at once despair ; but with humility and patience wait for the heavenly visitation ; for God is able to give thee back again more ample consolation " (Bk. ii. ch. 9).

V

THE MYSTERY OF TEMPTATION

"And when the devil had ended all the temptation, he departed from him for a season."
—St. Luke iv. 13.

It is clear that the words 'tempt' and 'temptation' ($\pi\epsilon\iota\rho\acute{a}\zeta\epsilon\iota\nu$, $\pi\epsilon\iota\rho\alpha\sigma\mu\acute{o}\varsigma$), are used in Scripture in two senses.

Sometimes they are used for the various forms of suffering, whether of bodily pain, mental distress, or outward circumstances,—'mind, body, or estate,' —which test our moral courage, and put our religious temper to the proof. Thus our Lord in the Parable of the Sower says of the shallow-ground hearers that "in time of temptation they fall away,"—clearly alluding to the persecutions of the world. So St. Paul speaks of his labours at Ephesus (Acts xx. 19) as having been accompanied with "many tears and temptations which befel him by the lying in wait of the Jews." Similarly St. Peter (1 P. iv. 12) writes: "Beloved, think it not strange concerning the fiery trial which is to try you" (πειρασμός), etc. And, not to accumulate examples, in Rev. iii. 10, to Philadelphia it is said: "I will keep thee from the hour of temptation, which shall come upon all the world, to try them that dwell upon the earth" (πειρασμός, πειράζειν).

In other passages the same words are used in a different sense; they do not describe external persecutions, nor bodily or mental pain, but the allurements and enticements of a spirit of evil working upon the baser appetites or leanings of the human character. Thus in a famous passage of St. James (i. 13): "Let no man say when he is tempted, I am tempted of God: for God cannot be tempted with evil, neither tempteth he any man: but every man is tempted, when he is drawn away of his own lust, and enticed." Here it is the inner allurement of evil working upon the frailty and corruption of the human spirit, which is spoken of as 'temptation.' Equally clear is the meaning of St. Paul in 1 Tim. vi. 9: "But they that will ($βουλόμενοι$) be rich fall into temptation and a snare, and into many foolish and hurtful lusts," etc.

It seems clear that modern religious language makes a wide distinction between these two ideas, although they are brought together under one head by the usage of Scripture. To us there seems all the difference in the world between the persecutions which 'try' a martyr, and the 'temptations' of vanity, greed, or lust which allure the inner soul. With us a trial is one thing, a temptation another. We observe also that in the wilderness our Lord was really 'tempted,' and not merely 'tried.' All through His public life He underwent suffering and trial: but, as a rule, He was free from the enticing suggestions of the evil one. May we not say that this immunity was the consequence of His victory in the wilderness? There and then He had met the enticements of the devil, and had dealt decisively with his plausible suggestions of evil. "The devil" therefore "departed from him for a season" ($\mathring{a}\chi\rho\iota\ \kappa\alpha\iota\rho o\hat{v}$). Only once or twice again in His holy life do we find indications in the words and action of our Saviour, that He was conscious of a deliberate attempt of the evil one to mislead His judgment, or to surprise Him (if it were possible) into a deviation from the absolute standard of right. You remember, when the last and tragic visit

MYSTERY OF TEMPTATION 85

to Jerusalem drew near, and our Lord broke to His disciples the prospect of His Passion and death, how St. Peter took Him and rebuked Him for speaking so,—it sounded like a confession of failure and despair. Then, we read,— " When he had turned about and looked on his disciples, he rebuked Peter, saying, Get thee behind me, Satan: for thou savourest not the things that be of God, but the things that be of men " (Mark viii. 33). Is it not clear that the pleading, human, trustful voice of St. Peter stirred in our Lord's human spirit an agony of recoil from the disappointment, failure, and dread anguish of the Passion, and that Satan was using that instant of agony to renew the attack upon His constancy? It was a renewal of the temptation in the wilderness.

Yet again, in Gethsemane, and again upon the Cross, Satan took advantage of the agony of His human spirit and the pains of His tortured body, to suggest thoughts of fear, or irresolution, or despair,—but in vain. He rests still upon the Father's love and purpose: " My father, if it be possible . . . nevertheless not my will, but thine be done." " My God, my God, why hast thou forsaken me?" Though all be ever so dark, and human strength is failing, and human friends are absent or helpless, still He is God's and God is His. Into His hands, in the darkness and agony of death, He can commend His human spirit.

So far as the sacred narrative informs us, these are the only occasions when the fiery darts of evil suggestion invaded the Saviour's soul,—to be instantly quenched and repelled by the shield of faith and of prayer. Trials indeed were His and unceasing sorrows, through the bigotry and malice of the educated class, through the ignorance and instability of the crowd, through the dulness of His disciples, and through the weariness and painfulness of His long pilgrimage of love, which the peaceful sojourns at Bethany only throw into deeper relief.

> Quaerens me sedisti lassus
> Redemisti crucem passus.

It is expressly remarked of the scribes and Pharisees, who endeavoured to entangle Him in His talk: "This they said tempting him." And it is of all these various sorrows and privations that He speaks Himself under the term 'temptation': "Ye are they which have continued with me in my temptations" (Luke xxii. 28).

It appears to be worth enquiring how it came to pass that in Holy Scripture there is what seems to us so strange a confusion between two different things—trials and temptations. Why is it that both are described quite commonly by the same term? Why is it that in many passages the two are so closely brought together, that it is not easy at once to tell whether the word (πείραζειν, πειρασμός, 'tempt,' 'temptation') refers to one class of sufferings or the other, to enticements to sin, or the storms of persecution? I refer to such passages as these: "My brethren, count it all joy when ye fall into divers temptations" (James i. 2); "Blessed is the man that endureth temptation" (*ib.* i. 12); or "There hath no temptation taken you but such as is common to man: but God is faithful, who will not suffer you to be tempted above that ye are able; but will with the temptation also make a way to escape, that ye may be able to bear it" (1 Cor. x. 13). How shall we account for what looks like a confusion of thought or of language? For indeed the two kinds of suffering seem so broadly contrasted. One is outward, the other inward. One is direct incitement to sin; the other commonly braces and invigorates the spirit. One appeals to the inclinations of our nature; the other is abhorrent to them. One allures, the other alarms. In one Satan comes as a creeping serpent, in the other as a roaring lion.

To find the answer to this question, is to acquaint ourselves with the peculiar view put forth in Holy Scripture of human nature and its temptations, and of the part taken therein by an evil spirit.

In the view of the New Testament writers everything is a temptation which tends to move the human spirit from its loyal obedience to the Will of God, which makes it doubt His love or desert His cause. Whether a Judas be ensnared by greed, or a David by lust, or a Peter be swept from his feet by fear of the soldiery, or a Demas by loving this present world, or the Christians of Thessalonica or Corinth are persecuted by their unbelieving neighbours,—all these attacks of the forces of evil, whether they be the crafts or the assaults of the devil, are included alike in the term temptation. And there is justification for this view. It matters not to the powers of evil whether we are seduced into wrong-doing by the allurements of sense, or the promptings of vanity or pride,—or driven by terror of persecution to deny the Lord that bought us,—or worn down by bodily pain and mental anguish until, soured and hardened, we doubt God's goodness and cease to love and pray. It matters not to Satan, so long as you cease to serve God, and leave the narrow and heavenward path, whether you have been misled by the phantom of pleasure, or browbeaten by the hangman fear. In either case you are tempted, and you go wrong—nay more, in both cases the appeal is made by our spiritual tempter to the lowest impulses of our nature. When pleasure is the bait, our animal

MYSTERY OF TEMPTATION 91

instincts respond to the stimulus. When terror assails, the instinct of self-preservation is stirred; we become recreants to principle, and throw conscience overboard, to save our skin.

But we have need to go back in imagination to the New Testament times, before we can do justice to the New Testament idea of 'temptation.' The danger to a primitive Christian of dishonouring the Christian name by inconsistent living was perhaps less great than now, because, the Christian Church being then a small body in the midst of surrounding heathenism, discipline was stronger, the rules of the Christian life more definite, and the power of the social motive immeasurably greater.[1] But the tempta-

[1] In *Acts* (ix. 2; xix. 9, 23) Christianity is significantly termed *The Way*, *i.e.* a definite rule of life. Compare the remarks of Adam Smith on the disciplinary influence of small religious bodies (*Wealth of N.*, Bk. V. Ch. i.).

tion to a Christian of those days to desert the faith under the pressure of persecution,—sometimes the petty torments of social exclusion, sometimes the merciless attacks of mob violence, —was terribly real and perilous. Do we sufficiently remember that two great Epistles (1 *Peter* and *Hebrews*) as well as the *Apocalypse* itself, were written avowedly with the object of steadying the hearts of persecuted believers and churches, who were wavering in their loyalty to Christ under the strain of increasing cruelty? No wonder that in those evil times the words 'tempt' and 'temptation' were used indifferently whether for the secret 'crafts' or overt 'assaults' of the tempter. It matters not to him, nor is it less serious for the Church, whether one is led to betray the Cross by the intoxication of passion within, or by menace from without. In either case, we have been tested, and have proved traitors to the Lord.

But, further, this wider use of the term Temptation is justified by the fact that all through the New Testament Satan is spoken of as the agent of evil to the body as well as the soul. Our trials and tribulations, as well as our enticements to sin, are attributed to his malice. Our Lord Himself employs language which at least implies His acquiescence in this belief of His day: "And ought not this woman, being a daughter of Abraham, whom Satan hath bound, lo, these eighteen years, be loosed from this bond on the sabbath day?" (Luke xiii. 16). St. Paul uses similar language to describe his 'thorn in the flesh,' doubtless a bodily ailment (2 Cor. xii. 7):[1] "And lest I should be exalted above measure . . . there was given to me a thorn in the flesh, the messenger of Satan to

[1] With which compare *Gal.* iv. 14: τὸν πειρασμόν μου ὑμῶν τὸν ἐν τῇ σαρκί μου, "My bodily malady which tried your faith in me."

buffet me, lest I should be exalted above measure." This idea is equally implied in the same Apostle's language (1 Cor. v. 5) in speaking of excommunication: "To deliver such an one unto Satan for the destruction of the flesh, that the spirit may be saved in the day of the Lord Jesus." Here 'to deliver up to Satan' means to expose them to the peril of physical hurt and misfortune, unhelped and unprotected by the prayers and sacraments of the Church, so that by fear and chastisement they might be brought to repentance. And this further explains 1 Tim. i. 20: "Of whom is Hymenæus and Alexander; whom I have delivered unto Satan" (*i.e.* have excommunicated) "that they may learn not to blaspheme." Even plainer still is the same meaning in 1 Thess. ii. 18, where St. Paul is excusing his delay in revisiting Thessalonica: "Wherefore we would have come unto you, even I Paul, once and again; but Satan hindered us." The hindrances that occurred, whether they arose out of sickness or other external circumstance, are set down to the malice of Satan, who was always for obstructing so good a cause.[1] I think it must be conceded that this view of Satanic agency prevailed among the Jews of Apostolic and of Gospel days. How early, and in what manner the belief had rooted itself in popular Judaism, I cannot here pause to enquire. It is however noteworthy that we read in Genesis (xxii. 1) that "God did tempt Abraham," and there is no mention made of a spiritual intermediary; whereas in the book of Job (ch. 1), the trial or temptation of the patriarch while permitted by God, is actually executed by the mediation of the evil

---

[1] St. Chrysostom's comment on *Acts* xx. 9 (when Eutychus fell down during St. Paul's preaching at Troas) is: "At this point the devil disturbed their happy gathering."

one, this concession of power to Satan being set forth in a highly dramatic manner.[1] From this difference between the narrative of Genesis and of Job, may we not infer that a change of view had come in between the dates of the two documents concerned, and that it was a still further and later development of Hebrew belief to think of diabolic agency as being involved in all cases of bodily suffering? But observe, that if the elaboration of this belief was relatively late, it was adopted (like most of the Jewish opinions of the time) into the belief of the Christian Church.[2] Nor is there anything in the idea itself to jar with

---

[1] Compare the dramatic passage in 1 K. xxii. 19-22. Such highly poetical language ought not to be pressed by theologians too far.

[2] Where it gave rise to the practice of exorcism in Baptism, and other like ceremonies. The old Greek Baptismal service is full of such elements.

MYSTERY OF TEMPTATION

our fundamental belief in God's mercy and power. If evil angels exist, it is certain that they exist only by the permission of divine wisdom and love, and they can act upon man and upon nature only just in so far as they are permitted by the One sovereign Ruler of all. Their power is limited and controlled, and is to cease. "God shall bruise Satan under your feet shortly" (R. xvi. 20). There is nothing inconceivable in the notion of God's employment of Satanic agency even for the chastisement of His own children, just as He confessedly uses the wicked of this world for the same purpose (Is. x. 3). Satanic agency, then, however we may conceive of it, is only permitted, is controlled, is transitory. Satan has been virtually overcome already by the Saviour, who is our Representative. It remains for us to do our part by His grace, until the appointed end, the assured and ultimate victory. "For we wrestle not against flesh and blood, but against principalities, against powers, against the rulers of the darkness of this world, against spiritual wickedness in high places" (*i.e.* in the sphere of the invisible, Eph. vi. 12).

Let me make two remarks before I end; one is on a point of interpretation; the other, of practice.

1. The line of thought we have ventured to pursue leads up to an interesting interpretation of the closing words of the Lord's prayer: "Lead us not into temptation, but deliver us from the evil one." There is now no doubt among scholars that this is the only possible translation. The petition as a whole refers to sufferings of body and circumstances of 'trial' quite as much as to inner experiences of the soul, and the word 'temptation' is here employed in its widest New Testament sense. When then after

praying our Heavenly Father to spare us from troubles and temptations—in a word, from all trials that may be too much for our strength—we are taught to pray further that God would " rescue us from the evil one," is it not clear that Satan is viewed throughout as the enemy of man's whole nature, that he uses the pain of the body or the distress of the mind as a means of mischief, and that we are taught to pray to be delivered from his malign influence either by being spared the trial or by receiving divine help to overcome ?

2. We close with (I hope) a fresh perception of the spiritual nature and environment of man. We are citizens of two worlds, the seen and the unseen. Nay, rather, the two run up into one in our own religious consciousness, in the actual working out of life. Our handling of the things of time determines the destiny of eternity. All the awful

possibilities of human character, for good or for evil, are being developed as we deal with the seeming trifles of the hour. Each man's conflict between right and wrong, however secret or personal, is but a fragment of a vast, world-wide conflict whereof the original source and the ultimate issues are far out of the sight and ken of our human faculties; far beyond the horizon of earthly experience. Man is neither all body nor all spirit; he is both, and both at once. The evil in him is linked with all moral and spiritual evil outside and beyond him, not only in this world but in the world unseen. And, likewise, the good in him is linked with the eternal goodness and almighty power and unfailing love of God our Father, whose children we are; for by His Spirit we have been made members of the body of Christ, Who lived our life and took upon Him our flesh, and redeemed our whole humanity.

The humblest act of service now gains an eternal significance; our life is transfigured by rays of glory.

> Such is the bliss of souls serene,
> When they have sworn and steadfast mean,
> Counting the cost, in all to espy
> Their God, in all themselves deny.

VI

OUR LORD'S USE OF HOLY SCRIPTURE

"It is written."—St. Matt. iv. 4.

The study of our Lord's Temptation has drawn us into a number of serious questions both of doctrine and of duty. We have had to deal with the deep things of theology and of life. We have felt ourselves to be treading, indeed, on holy ground; for we have been trying to enter into the secret experiences of the Saviour's soul. But we have reason to believe that, in so doing, we have obeyed the guidance of the Spirit; for Christ Himself revealed this experience for our learning.

What then is the great and permanent lesson He would have us learn thereby?

I think we learn, above all else, from the history of our Lord's Temptation, that our safety amid whatever trials and temptations lies always in preserving a right attitude of the soul.

What is the right attitude of the soul? It is, in brief, an attitude of dutiful obedience. " Lord, what wilt thou have me to do?" "Thy will be done." This is the secret of our Lord's victory in each of the three temptations. In the first, He will not desire to end His fast by a miracle; He will await God's time for that: God's will be done. In the second, He will make no compromise with evil, in order to conciliate the favour of men. He will seek God's glory only. Come success or failure, God's will must be done. In the third, He will not permit Himself to rejoice in His unique powers; they are His for a purpose, and that purpose is the salvation of man and the glory of God. God's will alone shall be done.

But we may go further, and ask what means our Lord employed to maintain this perfect, this filial attitude of the soul towards the Heavenly Father. The means He employed were such as to make Him in this, as in all other things, our pattern.

(1) He held frequent communion with the Father by prayer and meditation. It was for this purpose mainly that He sought the forty days' sojourn in the wilderness. Happy for us, if, in the busiest and most anxious periods of our life, we maintain unbroken our intercourse by prayer with the Father in heaven.

(2) But also, the soul of our Saviour was steeped in the Old Testament Scripture. He knew its letter; He was full of its spirit. He who, in His

divine pre-existence is the Eternal Word of God; He who, as the Word made flesh, was the fulfilment of the Law and the Prophets; He, in His own human spirit was nourished and enlightened and upheld by the study of those inspired writings themselves. The Incarnate Word, in fulfilling the written word, found in that written word His direction and delight. Every passage in our Saviour's life, every crisis in His experience, testifies to His love and knowledge of Holy Scripture. This is nowhere more significant and emphatic than in the temptation in the wilderness.

Each reply of the Saviour to the tempter is taken from one and the same book of Scripture. Which is that? It is the book of Deuteronomy, a book which many a casual reader of the Old Testament has passed over as being less important, less original, than other books. It contains no striking narrative; it seems to add nothing new. It includes indeed some curious fragments of early annals, and it closes with some glorious pieces of old Hebrew poetry. But the main body of the book is made up of long discourses, supposed to be addressed by Moses to the Israelites shortly before his death. It is a volume of discourses, of sermons; and sermons, more quickly than most things in literature, grow out of date.

And yet every expert student is aware that Deuteronomy is the most spiritual book of the Old Testament. It breathes the spirit of the greatest prophets. Nowhere is there a higher conception of the nature and will of God, or a clearer view of love as the mainspring of obedience. In the book of Deuteronomy we come nearer than anywhere else in the Old Testament to the teaching of the New. And this is why our Lord loved the book, and used it so wonderfully.

For, apart from the use made of it in the Temptation, we find our Lord quoting Deuteronomy at least thrice. From Deut. xv. 11,—a passage well worth attentive study,—came our Lord's saying that "the poor ye have always with you." Another passage of Deuteronomy (vi. 4-9 : " Hear, O Israel : the Lord our God is one Lord : and thou shalt love the Lord thy God with all thine heart," etc.) was selected by later Israel for daily recitation by every pious Jew, as summing up in an inspired formula the essence of his faith and duty : and it is not a little remarkable that our Lord employs this passage on two occasions ; once when asked, " What is the great commandment in the law ?" (Matt. xxii. 37 ; Mk. xii. 29), and again in replying to the lawyer who enquired of Him, " What shall I do that I may inherit eternal life ?" (Lk. x. 25). Nor will readers of the Romans (x. 8 foll.) forget the magnificent use which St. Paul makes of that sublime text of Deut. xxx. 11 foll., which describes the spiritual indwelling of the law of God: "For this commandment which I command thee this day, it is not hidden from thee, neither is it far off. It is not in heaven, that thou shouldest say, Who shall go up for us to heaven, and bring it unto us, that we may hear it, and do it? Neither is it beyond the sea, that thou shouldest say, Who shall go over the sea for us, and bring it unto us, that we may hear it, and do it? But the word is very nigh unto thee, in thy mouth, and in thy heart, that thou mayest do it."

I venture therefore to-day, in view of our Lord's example, to urge upon members of the Church the necessity of a due acquaintance with the letter and the spirit of Holy Scripture. Observe that I say, both of the letter and the spirit. The knowledge of the letter is indeed of no value without the assimilation of its spirit. But we shall hardly be likely to learn and inwardly digest the teachings of Scripture without reading and marking its letter.

I

Never, perhaps, since the Reformation has the Bible been less read, less widely known among the mass of Christian people, than at this hour. What is the cause of this neglect? It is a very serious fact, and must be completely altered, if an enlightened and devout Christianity is ever again to recover and retain its hold upon the English people. In part the reason is found in the manifold and clamorous demands of other studies, and of the ephemeral press, upon general attention. In other words, we live so much in the present and the actual, that we have little time for things distant in time or interest, and certainly not for the indirect teachings (for such they are) of

Holy Scripture. Put in another form this means, that we are so much absorbed in things material that the ideal and the spiritual cease to have a compelling attraction for us. All this may be very largely true. But it would be at once more interesting and far more helpful if we could put our finger upon the immediate reasons for this neglect, and so suggest a remedy.

Now I think the average man of to-day feels a recoil from the study of Holy Scripture, and especially of the Old Testament, from two causes. In the first place, he feels dazed and confused by the multifariousness of Scripture. He expected to read a book, and he finds himself in a library. He is lost in the largeness and the variety of the whole literature. He needs a principle of selection, a point of view, some guidance through the seeming labyrinth. In the second place, he feels embarrassed by the prominence of the miraculous and wonderful in the narratives. His own experience of the common round of life in no way prepares him for such a situation. The ethical interest of Scripture impresses him indeed; and its biographies even delight him with their personal charm. But he is struck with an air of aloofness from ordinary life, an unreality, due to the prevalence of the miraculous. He is sorry that the presence of the spiritual should involve the emergence of the supernatural. For he craves for something that shall touch the deepest chords of his being,—the conscience and the will,—and bring heaven and earth together by the spell of moral sympathy.

II

If we have given at all a right diagnosis of the common indifference of the day, then I believe that in the book of Deuteronomy we have the very specific for the disease. The book so signally honoured by our Lord affords us just the help we want.

In the first place, it has been shown by recent research, to be not a secondary book, but a book of primary importance. It is no mere "second edition of the Law" or 'Deuteronomy' (as the LXX. by an inaccurate rendering of ch. xvii. 18 suggest). Rather, it is one of the freshest, most original, and even singular, of all the Old Testament books. Its very history is a romance. For most scholars now recognise in Deuteronomy the identical 'Book of the Law' which was found in the temple in the 18th year of King Josiah (2 Kings xxii.). We know how both king and people were stirred and alarmed by its perusal; how the reforms it enjoined were at once carried into effect and thus changed the character of Hebrew religion for ever, purifying and also centralising it; how the spirit of the book infused itself into all succeeding scriptures. For Deuteronomy breathes the lofty moral sentiments of an Hosea, a Micah, an Isaiah. It embodies their spirit in a style suited to everyday life and to the average Hebrew. But if prophetic in spirit, it is not so in its form. For it avoids the passionate moods, the daring imagery of the prophets, and expresses itself in prose. That prose is indeed of the noblest and most serious kind : it throbs with emotion, but its style is that of a refined and chastened rhetoric. We know not who was the author, though we can fix his date within narrow limits. Perhaps he wrote it in the evil days of king Manasseh, when in secret companionship with other faithful souls he kept alive his own faith and theirs by depicting in these pages the spirit and conduct of an ideal Israelite. The book makes no pretence of being *written* by Moses. It only professes to be a record, by a later pen, of the last exhortations addressed by Moses to Israel at the close of the wilderness wanderings. There is nothing outwardly original in the book. It borrows its history from older documents which we can yet trace amid the highly composite narratives of the Pentateuch. It selects its rules of law from older codes. The magnificent poems that close the book come, no doubt, from older national collections. But that which is original in Deuteronomy is the lofty conception of God's purity, patience, and love, and of Israel's relation to his God. For Israel is God's child, and God is a Father to Israel. Moreover, unlike many of the books of the Old Testament, Deuteronomy has undergone little or no revision since it left its author's hand. It stands in our Bible substantially in the form in which it was found so strangely in the year 621 B.C. Its very history, as we said, is a romance. And by its date and character it steps at once into prominence, as a central book of Holy Scripture. Every book of the Old Testament takes its place as viewed in relation to Deuteronomy. It has none of the crudity of thought and expression which we note in the older portions of the Pentateuch ; it has none of their anthropomorphism, little of their imperfect and provisional morality. As compared again with later books like Ezekiel and the later priestly codes, Deuteronomy is less Levitical, less careful of ceremonial. It is a manual not for priests, but for the lay-folk, to teach the average Hebrew his duties. And so Deuteronomy becomes a sort of touchstone of Old Testament Scripture: we can trace the development of Jewish literature by the way in which it led up to Deuteronomy, or afterwards was influenced by Deuteronomy, whether in its characteristic phrases, or (still more) in its significant conceptions of Israel's relation to God. It is not too much to say, that the right appreciation of the place of Deuteronomy in Jewish literature, has given us a priceless key to the understanding of the origin and growth and meaning of the Old Testament books. We can now read them with a sense of their orderly sequence, their historical development.

But I alluded also to the revulsion from the miraculous in the temper of the average man. Now the Deuteronomist shows no inclination to revel in the merely marvellous. His interest in the wonderful history of the Hebrews is purely ethical. The marvels of the Exodus, the deliverances in the wilderness, the strange vicissitudes that had made "a Syrian ready to perish" (Deut. xxvi. 5) into a thriving and populous nation,—all these are dwelt upon again and again, in varying terms, only to enforce the one central idea of God's electing love, and Israel's corresponding obligation of loving and trustful obedience. Just as, in the legal portions of Deuteronomy, precisely those details of law seem to be selected which make for mercy and kindness, both to man and beast,—so the selection from the history of Israel seems made with the view of exhibiting Jehovah not as a God of nature, but of Providence and Grace. Deuteronomy was a manual of practical theology for the plain man. It leavens every department of his life and conduct with the principle of divine love, so that duty itself is transfigured into privilege, and privilege is made equivalent to duty, in the light of God's loving kindness. Now it is precisely in this light, when we begin to grasp the ethical side of true theology, and feel drawn to God by the disclosures of His love, that there dawns upon us the reasonableness even of miracle, the *naturalness* (if we may so phrase it) of the supernatural. For true religion being always the unveiling of God's character and the working of His love, it is hard to see how His love and power could have been disclosed to us in the way of grace as contrasted with nature without the accompaniment of much that is marvellous to man. There can be no true religion, we assume, without mystery; for man is not equal with God. On the other hand, few things are more destructive to religion than to subordinate its ethical and spiritual instincts to the mere emotion of wonder. Christianity is not, nor can be made to be, a mere marvel-monger. "Except ye see signs and wonders ye will not believe," said Christ, reprovingly. "The Jews require a sign" (complains St. Paul), "and the Greeks seek after wisdom: but we preach Christ crucified": *i.e.* it is the moral grandeur and unique wisdom of Jesus Christ which constitute the central wonder of the Gospel. To exalt the marvellous in Christianity above the ethical was precisely the error of Simon Magus when he sought to purchase the power of communicating the miraculous gift of tongues (Acts viii. 18, 19). But the error is deeply seated in human nature, as witness the devotions of our Lady of Lourdes both in their origin and in their developments.

III

So then this book of Deuteronomy, both as a central and illuminating landmark in Jewish literature and as the loftiest embodiment of Old Testament theology and ethics, assumes a singular value for the modern reader of Scripture. It idealizes Judaism : it shows the essential meaning of Judaism as a religion for the individual and the nation. It lifts to the highest level the provisional and progressive morality of the Old Testament. From its Pisgah heights of spirituality we can discern the advent of Him who is the Lord our righteousness, in whom both the law and the prophets are fulfilled.

It is just because the Old Testament appears to many to lack this advanced and concentrated ethical fervour, this sense of Divine compassion, this conception of man's loving relations to God, that men seem disinclined to approach it. The whole of the Old Testament assumes a new meaning for us in the light of this interesting book; for it affords a clue to the development of religion among the Hebrews; it points us along the line of their progressive morality; and it no less certainly sums up for us the religious teaching of their great prophetic order.

Certain I am that if we are to be emancipated from a hard and gross materialism, if as individuals we are to live by faith, and as a nation and empire to cultivate true ideals of righteousness, of responsibility and compassion, it must be by returning to Holy Scripture with enlightened, devout and serious study. It is not a question of one literature being inspired and another uninspired. It is not a question of mere authority. The question is, What is the literature, where is the written word in which the human conscience—individual or collective—finds the loftiest appeals, the most simple and searching challenge, the most powerful spur and guidance? If these are what we seek—and nothing we need so much—they are found pre-eminently in holy writ. They are found elsewhere, in their degree, wherever man's heart has borne articulate witness to ethical truth ; but nowhere are they so concentrated in force, so cumulative in effect, so authoritative in spiritual claim, as in Scripture. The neglect of Scripture is a painful token of national decline. We were once, we English, a Bible-reading, a Bible-loving people. We too proudly deem that our fathers worshipped the letter of Scripture overmuch; we profess to prefer its spirit. We have need to set ourselves, far more than we are doing, to learn its letter, before we aspire to evince its spirit and purpose.

As a nation, as individuals, we are beset with terrible temptations. I have tried to show that our temptations are no other than those which assailed our Lord. We must meet them as He met them, in a spirit of filial trust and obedience, in a spirit of prayer, and with a conscience braced and purified by Holy Scripture. We must wield against the tempter the sword of the Spirit, which is the Word of God; we must say, as Christ said, and with due sense of its ethical meaning, "It is written,—It is written,—It is written."

www.ingramcontent.com/pod-product-compliance
Lightning Source LLC
Chambersburg PA
CBHW070501100426
42743CB00010B/1715